First World War:

We will remember them

D1324047

▲ King George and the Prince of Wales in a Rolls in Flanders.

▲ Germans arrive at a deserted trench.

IF ENGLAND FALLS YOU FALL!

Every Man of you must go, as We, too, Must Go!

SIR RIDER HAGGARD in St. John, August, 1914

▲ Canadian poster.

A CVP Book
Copyright © Atlantic Europe Publishing 2010

Author
Brian Knapp, BSc, PhD

Editor
Gillian Gatehouse

Researcher
Lisa Magloff, MSc

Designed and produced by
Atlantic Europe Publishing

Senior Designer
Adele Humphries, BA, PGCE

Printed in China by
WKT Company Ltd

**First World War: We will remember them
– Curriculum Visions
A CIP record for this book is
available from the British Library**

Paperback ISBN 978 1 86214 669 3

Picture credits
All photographs are from the Library of Congress Picture Library except the following: (c=centre t=top b=bottom l=left r=right)
Imperial War Museum pages Cover, 6–7, 20–21, 26–27, 30t, 30b, 31, 33, 34–35, 36–37 (all), 45 (soldier).
The publishers have made their best endeavours to contact all copyright holders for material published in this book.

Acknowledgements
The publishers would like to thank Stella Wood.

This product is manufactured from sustainable managed forests. For every tree cut down at least one more is planted.

Contents

Words in **BOLD CAPITALS** are further explained in the glossary on page 47.

Note, at this time what is now the Republic of Ireland, was part of Britain. The word Britain is therefore used as a shorthand for "The British Isles", whose islands were the "Mother Country" to the British Empire of colonies and dominions around the world.

Note also that this book deals only with the Western Front so that events can be covered in some detail.

▲ Troops marching through Flanders, an area that was once a forest.

▲ British recruiting poster.

▲ Horse pulling a lorry out of the Flanders mud.

We will remember them…

This is the story of the First World War. It was the first war ever to affect all continents. It was meant to be the war to end all wars. It was not.

If you go around the country, no matter where you go, you will find, in parish, city or borough, an upright slab of stone with names of local people (picture ①, page 44) carved on it in neat rows. Many of these memorials are in the shape of a cross. Some of the largest, like the national memorial called the Cenotaph, in London's Whitehall, are shaped more like tall coffins. They are completely unique.

If you go to any of these memorials on the 11th hour of the 11th day of the 11th month of any year, you will find people gathered there, holding wreaths made of poppies. There will be people holding flags belonging to the **ROYAL BRITISH LEGION**. Then, when the hour strikes, all these people, and people all over the country, will stop whatever they are doing. They will stop driving, stop working, stop learning. They will stand, or sit in complete silence for 2 minutes.

Then, in the silence, a distant cannon might be heard and a single bugler might blow a baleful tune known as the Last Post.

In the short service that follows, one of the readers will say these words:

> "They shall grow not old, as we that are left grow old;
> Age shall not weary them, nor the years condemn
> At the going down of the sun and in the morning
> We will remember them."

All of these memorials, the service of remembrance, the poem, the poppies of the wreaths and the flags are all part of our nation giving just a moment's thought to the terrible events of a war like no other before or since.

… and it happened just a century ago.

▼ ① The Worcestershires going into action.

▶ ② The poppy is the symbol of the First World War because it was the first thing to flower over the battlefields after the war.

The terrible war

The First World War was called 'the terrible war', not simply because of the number of dead, but because of the terrible conditions it was fought in.

The First World War (also known as the Great War, World War I, WWI) was meant to be the 'war to end all wars'. Of course we know it wasn't. It did not even have the most casualties.

In the First World War the figures for Britain and her **ALLIES** were: dead: 9.6 million; wounded: 12.8 million (picture ①).

▼ ① **Wounded British troops returning from the battlefield.**

Forces' casualties for Germany and her allies: 8.0 million; wounded: 8.8 million. British and allies' deaths were higher than German and allies' deaths.

During the Second World War about 11 million German, Italian and Japanese troops and civilians were killed, while about 60 million British and allied troops and civilians were killed, including those in Russia, in concentration camps and who died from starvation.

In both wars, the people trying to restore peace paid a heavier price than those who caused the war, and quite often civilians paid a higher price than troops.

The terrible war

Why, then, was the First World War called the 'terrible war'? Well, it was due to the indescribably ghastly conditions in which soldiers fought – and the fact that no one seemed to care. The story of the terrible war is told in the following pages...

On the verge of war

Britain still ruled an empire – and, with the world's largest navy, it ruled the waves. What could go wrong?

You can't understand the war unless you know what was going on just before it.

In 1914 British people had enjoyed great prosperity for more than a century. The **BRITISH EMPIRE** was still the largest in the world and British industry was still the envy of other countries. Although there had been many wars involving Britain, they had all been far from home. And we had won them all. People still remembered Admiral Horatio Nelson at the Battle of Trafalgar, and the Duke of Wellington at the Battle of Waterloo. They were all great victories.

▼ ① **The coronation of King George V as emperor in New Delhi, India, 1911.**

As far as most people in Britain were concerned, everything was fine. **BRITANNIA** still ruled the waves. But it was not fine, for events were about to unfold that would shatter the lives of many people across the world. War was in the air, and it was coming closer to home – but no-one was listening.

Leading to war

In 1914 news of events in Europe did not really interest British people because Britain, as an island, thought of itself as completely safe from attack.

As it happened, most of the kings and queens of Europe were related. For example, the Kaiser (King) of Germany was the cousin of King George V of Britain (picture ①). This gave the false impression that, if any problems arose, one king would talk to another and sort out the mess. People thought it would keep Europe a safer place. It did not. It had the opposite effect.

Assassination

Some people across Europe wanted to overthrow the idea of monarchs and democracy by setting off bombs. They were known as anarchists. They thought that if only they could kill the king of a country, it might turn one country against another and that might bring down the whole of Europe.

They were right (picture ②). It would happen because most countries of Europe had treaties which said that if one was attacked, others would come to their aid. It was meant to make things safer. It turned out to be a recipe for disaster.

◀ ② **The First World War was started by the assassination of Archduke Franz Ferdinand, heir to the Austrian empire, by a Serbian student.**

Weblink: www.CurriculumVisio

Your country needs YOU

Britain was suddenly faced with war, but it only had a small army. Something had to be done.

Britain was one of the most powerful countries in the world and it had the world's largest navy. That was because the British Isles are islands and all of its colonies and **DOMINIONS** were reached by ship.

The main worry had always been defending shipping routes using

convoys. As a result, Britain had a tiny army which was only used to go to trouble-spots in the empire. But when Germany began to advance across Europe, it was clear that a massive British army would be needed to support the French and other European countries in danger of invasion.

The problem was how to get an army together quickly. Lord Kitchener was a former army commander and famous for his campaigns in Africa. He predicted a long war and one in which millions of men would be needed. At that time, such huge numbers were undreamt of.

Because Lord Kitchener was one of the most respected and popular men in Britain, when a massive campaign to swell the army did finally get under way, it seemed right to use him to get volunteers to join. This was done by one of the most famous poster campaigns of all time. You can see variations of it on these pages.

TO MY PEOPLE.

At this grave moment in the struggle between my people and a highly organised enemy who has transgressed the Laws of Nations and changed the ordinance that binds civilized Europe together, I appeal to you.

I rejoice in my Empire's effort, and I feel pride in the voluntary response from my Subjects all over the world who have sacrificed home, fortune, and life itself, in order that another may not inherit the free Empire which their ancestors and mine have built.

I ask you to make good these sacrifices.

The end is not in sight. More men and yet more are wanted to keep my Armies in the Field, and through them to secure Victory and enduring Peace.

In ancient days the darkest moment has ever produced in men of our race the sternest resolve.

I ask you, men of all classes, to come forward voluntarily and take your share in the fight.

In freely responding to my appeal, you will be giving your support to our brothers, who, for long months, have nobly upheld Britain's past traditions, and the glory of her Arms.

George R.I.

The most striking posters showed Kitchener pointing straight towards the reader. It was probably this, rather than anything else, that persuaded many young men and even schoolboys, to turn up at recruiting stations all over the country so they could volunteer to help to save their country.

Many volunteers were under the accepting age of 16, but they falsified documents and got up to many other tricks just to be able to join. They thought it was going to be all good fun – and they wanted to be part of it.

RALLY ROUND THE FLAG

"WE MUST HAVE MORE ME[N]

Mr. JOSEPH DEVLIN, M.P.
AND THE
IRISH BRIGADE

" May every good fortune, success and blessing attend the colours of the Irish Brigade, whose valour, I hope, will be crowned with the laurels of glory worthily earned in the arena of a great conflict on behalf of a righteous cause . . . . .

" When they come back again, they will be welcomed not only as soldiers of the Allies, but as friends of liberty who have raised the dignity and prestige and glory of Ireland to a higher position than it ever occupied before . .

IRISHMEN
DO YOUR DUTY IN THIS RIGHTEOUS CAUSE AND
JOIN THE IRISH BRIGADE

YOUNG MEN
OF THE BAHAMAS

The British Empire is engaged in a Life and Death Struggle. Never in the History of England, never since the Misty Distant Past of 2,000 years ago, has our beloved Country been engaged in such a conflict as she is engaged in to-day.

To bring to nothing this mighty attack by an unscrupulous and well prepared foe, HIS MOST GRACIOUS MAJESTY KING GEORGE has called on the men of his Empire, MEN OF EVERY CLASS, CREED AND COLOUR, to

COME FORWARD TO FIGHT

that the Empire may be saved and the foe may be well beaten.

This call is to YOU, young man; not your neighbour, not your brother, not your cousin, but just YOU. SEVERAL HUNDREDS OF YOUR MATES HAVE COME UP, HAVE BEEN MEDICALLY EXAMINED AND HAVE BEEN PASSED AS "FIT."

What is the matter with YOU?

Put yourself right with your King; put yourself right with your fellowmen; put yourself right with yourself and your conscience.

ENLIST TO-DAY

The Happy Man Today is the Man at the Front

Royal Highlanders of Canada
Allied with the **BLACK WATCH**

Have Enlisted at their Armoury for Overseas Service

13th Bn. C.E.F.
Now in France

42nd Bn. C.E.F.
Now in England

AND THE

73rd Bn. C.E.F.
is now Mobilizing

JOIN THE 73rd. NOW

Apply at the Armoury of
ROYAL HIGHLANDERS OF CANADA
429 Bleury Street
MONTREAL

IF ENGLAND FALLS YOU FALL!

Every Man of you must go, as We, too, Must Go!

SIR RIDER HAGGARD in St. John, August, 1914

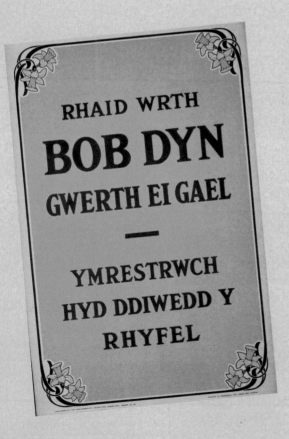

RHAID WRTH

BOB DYN

GWERTH EI GAEL

—

YMRESTRWCH

HYD DDIWEDD Y

RHYFEL

BULLDOG SOLDIERS' & SAILORS' CLUB

UNDER THE PERSONAL DIRECTION OF MAJ-GEN. SIR FRANCIS LLOYD, K.C.B. COMMANDING LONDON DISTRICT.

Chief Patroness: H·M· QUEEN AMÉLIE OF PORTUGAL.

1ST LIST OF PATRONS includes

The Lady Edmund Talbot   Admiral Sir Thomas Jackson, K.C.V.O.   Maj-Gen. F. W. B. Landon, C.B.   And many others.
Maj-Gen. Sir Alfred Turner, K.C.B.   Brigdr-Gen. Blackader, D.S.O, A.D.C.
Maj-Gen. H. L. Croker, C.B   Sir Frank Milner, K.C.B

CHAPEL ST EDGWARE Rd. W.

SOLDIERS' AND

THE BULLDOG

SAILORS' CLUB

"SOME

CLUB"

BUY A BULLDOG
on JUNE 16th
& make our Brave Boys comfortable.

PRESIDENT: THE MAYOR OF MARYLEBONE
ALL MONIES COLLECTED WILL BE PUT INTO THE HANDS OF TRUSTEES.

BANKERS—LLOYDS BANK, Ltd.

13

The 'pals' join up

One way to get more men to join up was to get people to enlist with their friends – their 'pals'. Then they could all laugh and joke with people they knew all the way to the front line.

Britain declared war on the 4th of August 1914. But it could only contribute 150,000 men, about a tenth of the forces of France or Germany.

The British government (as well as all other governments involved in the war) appealed to young men's sense of adventure, pride, patriotism, and, quite an important extra, the fact that

they would get a regular wage in the army. The government also tried to get women to encourage their husbands and boyfriends to join up. Later, women would be encouraged to join as nurses, and to support the war at home in many other ways, such as by knitting winter clothing for the men at the Front.

The campaign (see pages 10–13) run by Lord Kitchener was amazingly successful and by January 1916, more than one million British, and hundreds of thousands of Canadians, Anzacs (Australians and New Zealanders), and other members of the

Your Chums are fighting

Why aren't YOU?

C. J. Arthur:
"I was born in November 1898 so that when war was declared I was at school. I joined the School Cadet Battalion in 1914 and was appointed corporal.

At Whitsun, 1915, I told the Officer in command of cadets I was going to join up. "Good," he said. "How old do you want to be?"

We fixed things between us, and armed with a letter from him, I presented myself to the colonel of an infantry battalion which was just being formed, and on the strength of the letter I was appointed a lance-corporal and told to get my hair cut. I was in the army."

◄ ① Enlistment poster.

Empire had signed up (for example, a million Asians would fight in the war, and two all-Sikh battalions fought on the Western Front alone).

Propaganda

Propaganda is telling a story from just one side. By the end of 1914, more than 54 million propaganda posters had been printed encouraging people to enlist (picture ①).

One thing men were told was that it would be a quick and easy war, and that they would all be home for Christmas. It was also a quick and easy way to become a hero in the eyes of their loved ones. Another tactic was to give the press stories of horrible acts committed by the Germans and others. This was designed to make people hate the other side and see their own war as just. At the same time a just war made heroes of men. In a way it was seen as a kind of holy war.

The football battalion

At the start of the war there were 5,000 professional footballers. The football association publicly called for all un-married professional footballers to volunteer. This was a great coup for the army because most footballers were heroes. So they kept many of them together and formed the 17th Service (Football) Battalion of the Middlesex Regiment – the 'football battalion'.

Professional footballers were among the real heroes. Donald Bell, a footballer from Bradford City, was the first professional footballer to join up (picture ②). He took

▲ ② Donald Simpson Bell, VC.

part in the Battle of the Somme (see page 26), filling his pockets with hand grenades and attacking a machine gun. He was awarded the Victoria Cross for bravery. He was killed five days later.

Walter Tull was a black man who had played for Tottenham Hotspurs. He was part of the football battalion. He showed such promise that his senior officers wanted to send him to officer training school. At that time military regulations prohibited 'persons of colour' from being officers. With huge support, he became an officer all the same. He was an extremely popular and brave soldier. In 1918 he was hit by a bullet, and other soldiers risked their lives to get him back into the trenches. Unfortunately he died. Altogether twelve members of the Spurs football team were killed in the First World War.

Weblink: www.CurriculumVisions.com

A new kind of war – the Western Front

The Western Front was the largest front of the war, and where most British servicemen saw action.

After six weeks of training, most of the new recruits were sent to the Front (picture ①). Many companies marched first through their home towns, so their friends and family could give them a send off. But once at the Front, they quickly realised this war was not going to be easy, fun or quick.

The start of modern warfare

The First World War was like no war that had taken place before. It has been called the start of modern warfare.

The way the war was fought (called tactics) was still similar to those that had been used for hundreds of years – trenches, frontal attacks and calvary charges using horses. Yet it was also the first war in which aeroplanes, tanks, poison gas, **MINES**, submarines and machine guns were used.

What was the effect of combining old and new? Commanders did not yet know how to use the new weapons best, so they used them as they always had. But machine guns and shells (the 'bullets' from a large gun on wheels) were far more deadly than the single-shot rifles and cannon used before. The result was that using the old tactics caused vast numbers of extra casualties.

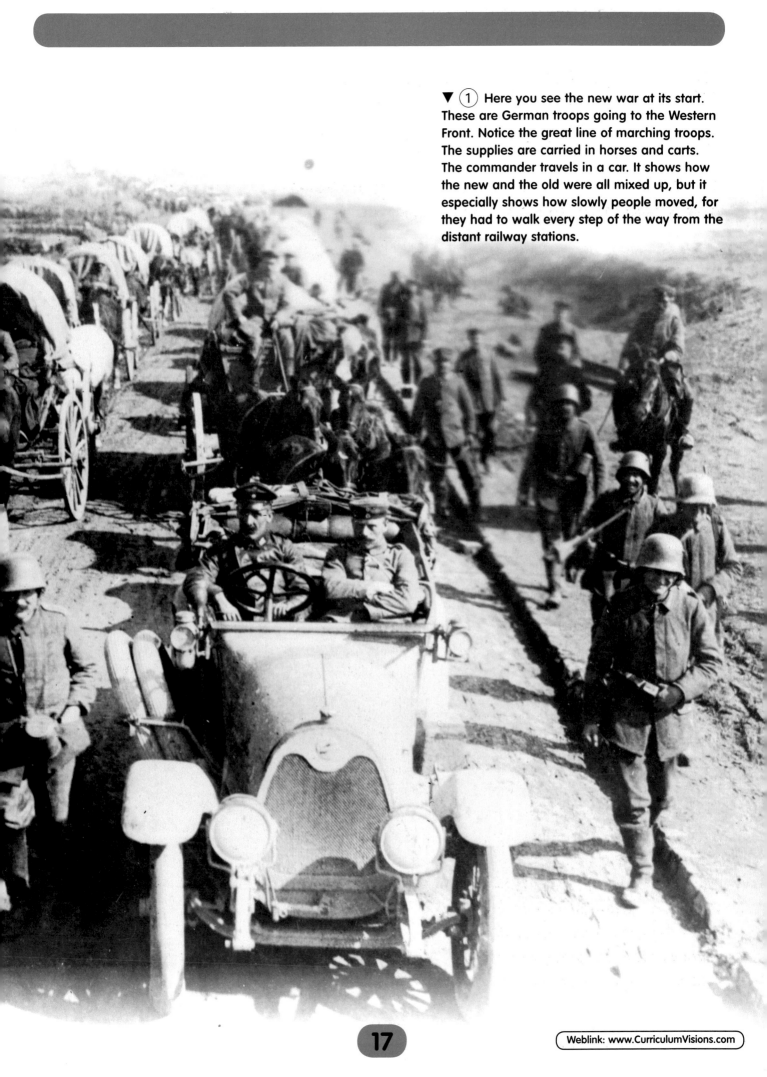

▼ ① Here you see the new war at its start. These are German troops going to the Western Front. Notice the great line of marching troops. The supplies are carried in horses and carts. The commander travels in a car. It shows how the new and the old were all mixed up, but it especially shows how slowly people moved, for they had to walk every step of the way from the distant railway stations.

Weblink: www.CurriculumVisions.com

Huge battles costing tens of thousands of lives would be fought simply to secure a few hundred metres of ground. Of course, to begin with, no-one knew this was going to happen.

The other thing about the First World War was that the two sides were very evenly matched. No one side was strong enough to win easily. If this had been a battle in the days of castles it would have been like a siege.

The Western Front

The place where most of the British troops fought was called the Western Front (the 'Front'). It was where Germany met France and Britain. The other front, the Eastern Front, was where Germany lined up against Russia.

The Western Front was a 700 kilometre-long line of trenches, and barbed wire that stretched from the English Channel to the Swiss frontier. Although the Front at first passed through many towns, villages and forests, within a year, the entire Western Front resembled a barren moonscape where nothing lived except soldiers and rats. The towns, villages and forests had been shelled to smithereens (picture ②).

▼▶ ② **Two views of the Western Front show it all. Complete destruction of the area where the forces met for four long years.**

ETAIN, NORTH-EAST OF VERDUN

NO-MANS LAND
ONCE A FOREST "IN FLANDERS FIELDS" X217

...ROYED BY THE GERMANS.

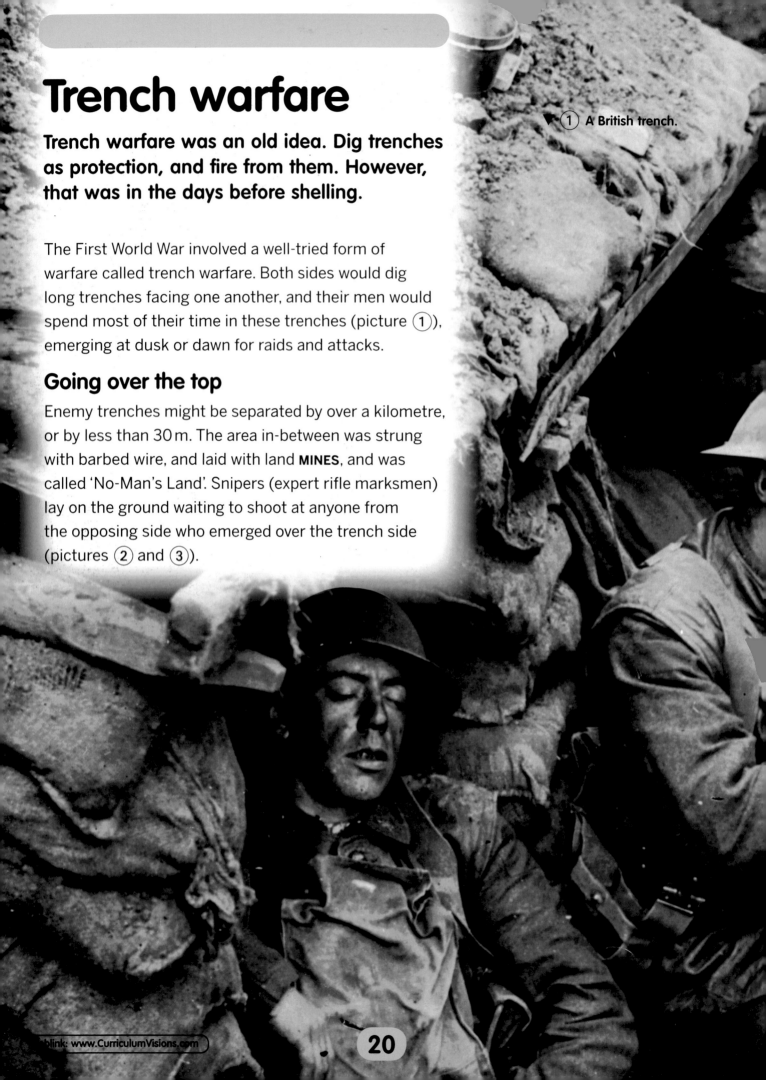

Trench warfare

Trench warfare was an old idea. Dig trenches as protection, and fire from them. However, that was in the days before shelling.

▼ ① A British trench.

The First World War involved a well-tried form of warfare called trench warfare. Both sides would dig long trenches facing one another, and their men would spend most of their time in these trenches (picture ①), emerging at dusk or dawn for raids and attacks.

Going over the top

Enemy trenches might be separated by over a kilometre, or by less than 30 m. The area in-between was strung with barbed wire, and laid with land **MINES**, and was called 'No-Man's Land'. Snipers (expert rifle marksmen) lay on the ground waiting to shoot at anyone from the opposing side who emerged over the trench side (pictures ② and ③).

▼ ② **German machine gun position.**

▼ ③ **A German sniper.**

The trenches provided cover against enemy bullets, but not against shells or hand grenades. 'Going over the top' was a term used to describe an attack – when soldiers used ladders to climb out of their trenches (going over the top of the trench) and then ran full pelt towards an enemy who were defending themselves with machine guns, mines and shells. It was all hopeless because there was no weapon that could be used to attack successfully. This is why, by October 1914, the Western Front was a **STALEMATE**, simply a killing ground fed by more and more troops from the rear. This is another thing that made it a terrible war.

▼ ④ German cavalry approach an abandoned British trench.

Each big push would cost the lives of thousands, or even tens of thousands of men. And even then advances were measured in metres.

Once a trench had been abandoned (picture ④) or taken over, the retreating forces would just move to a trench a few hundred metres back – making it necessary to start all over again.

A day in the trenches

Fighting was rare at night because no-one could see what they were doing. But everyone was woken an hour before dawn. This was called 'stand-to'. Dawn raids were very common, so this was a dangerous time and everyone had bayonets fixed to their rifles.

To prove they were still fighting fit and to relieve the boredom, troops then fired at the enemy. Neither side could see what they were doing. It was known as the morning hate, and it had little effect other than to keep men busy.

Then it was time for breakfast and in many places both sides observed an unofficial truce while the food wagons reached the lines.

For the rest of the day it was a matter of finding things to do, such as repairing the boards that kept men's feet out of the water, emptying the toilet buckets and cleaning guns. Most men wrote letters home during the day.

As dusk approached, everyone knew this was a danger time, so stand-to was observed again.

As soon as it was dark, there were things that could be done. Men were sent up into no-man's land to lay mines, add barbed wire and so on. Some men were sent to lie in hollows close to the enemy lines. These were called listening posts and they were very dangerous

▼ ⑤ Most of the time was spent waiting. This was not too bad in summer, but in winter the trenches would fill with ice-cold water. It was common to shave heads to avoid hair becoming infested with nits and lice.

trips. The idea was to overhear the plans of the enemy.

The first day in a trench was the deadliest for each new soldier. They didn't know the routine and they were curious about no-man's land. They often peeped over the trench and were killed by snipers.

If soldiers survived being killed by bullets, they were just as likely to die from disease. The trenches were infested with rats, and most men had lice (picture ⑤). Lice caused Trench Fever, something that might take three months to get over. Trench Foot was a fungus that grew on the surface of feet that were continually wet and cold. Sometimes it would cause **GANGRENE** and then the leg might have to be amputated. In winter, soldiers suffered frostbite.

Add to all this two further problems: the stench of dead bodies and human waste. That was another reason it was called the terrible war.

23

Thinking of you…

Families were separated for years. Families did not know what was happening to their loved ones. So, as something to do, many women bought and collected special war postcards. Many were never sent to the Front, but kept at home.

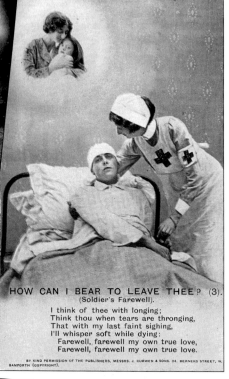

HOW CAN I BEAR TO LEAVE THEE? (1).
(Soldier's Farewell).

How can I bear to leave thee?
One parting kiss I give thee;
And then whate'er befalls me,
I go where honour calls me.
Farewell, farewell my own true love.
Farewell, farewell my own true love.

BY KIND PERMISSION OF THE PUBLISHERS, MESSRS. J. CURWEN & SONS, 24, BERNERS STREET, W.

HOW CAN I BEAR TO LEAVE THEE? (2).
(Soldier's Farewell).

Ne'ermore may I behold thee,
Or to this heart enfold thee;
With spear and pennon glancing,
I see the foe advancing.
Farewell, farewell my own true love,
Farewell, farewell my own true love.

BY KIND PERMISSION OF THE PUBLISHERS, MESSRS. J. CURWEN & SONS, 24, BERNERS STREET, W.

HOW CAN I BEAR TO LEAVE THEE? (3).
(Soldier's Farewell).

I think of thee with longing;
Think thou when tears are thronging,
That with my last faint sighing,
I'll whisper soft while dying:
Farewell, farewell my own true love,
Farewell, farewell my own true love.

BY KIND PERMISSION OF THE PUBLISHERS, MESSRS. J. CURWEN & SONS, 24, BERNERS STREET, W.
BAMFORTH (COPYRIGHT).

There's not an hour that passes
Throughout the livelong day,
But brings back tender memories
Of my loved ones far away.

FRED⁰ SPURGIN.

TO MY LOVED ONES FAR AWAY

In fancy, dear, I seem to see,
Your face, that's all the
world to me,
Tho' absent from each others-
My heart is yours, side,
whate'er betide.

FRED⁰ SPURGIN

TO ONE WHO'S ALL THE WORLD TO ME

I long to be with you, dear Heart,
But countless miles us sever,
So send this token just to prove
A love that lasts for ever.

FRED⁰ SPURGIN

FROM MY HEART

The First World War was not long after the death of Queen Victoria and the way that people felt was still very much part of Victorian times. Victorians were very sentimental people and produced what we would now think of as very 'flowery' cards.

The war brought back many sentimental songs and cards. These postcards with poems were popular at home. Many of the poems used on these cards were written in Victorian times (picture ①) and were well-known in music halls and elsewhere.

THE BRAVEST, THE BEST (2).

England's Navy, British Soldiers true,
Comrade to comrade, fight for I and you,
Shoulder to shoulder, firm to the test,
Pride of the whole world, the bravest, the best.

THE BRAVEST, THE BEST (1).

Many brave men have left children and wives,
Gone to the front at the risk of their lives.
There's been a parting, there's been a tear,
Good-bye, my darling, for me have no fear.
My country is calling, I cannot stay,
If God is willing, I'll come back some day.
You will be proud of the man you love true,
Who fought for his country his duty to do.

THE BRAVEST, THE BEST (3).

Battles are raging, hearts beat with despair,
Children are praying for fathers out there.
Oft shall we hear them pleadingly say:
"Mother, where is Dad? Won't he come home some day?"
Then midst broken sobs the truth she will tell,
Of how like a hero their father had fell.
Won't they be proud of their brave Daddy,
Who fought for his country his duty to do.

THE VACANT CHAIR (1).

We shall meet, but we shall miss him, there will be one vacant chair;
We shall linger to caress him, while we breathe our ev'ning pray'r.
When a year ago we gathered, joy was in his mild blue eye,
But a golden chord is severed, and our hopes in ruin lie.

THE VACANT CHAIR (2)

At our fireside, sad and lonely, often will the bosom swell
At remembrance of the story how our noble Father fell;
How he strove to bear our banner through the thickest of the fight;
And uphold our Country's honour, in the strength of manhood's might.

THE VACANT CHAIR (3).

True, they tell us wreaths of glory evermore will deck his brow.
But this soothes the anguish only sweeping o'er the heart strings now.
Sleep to-day, O early fallen, in thy green and narrow bed,
Dirges from the pine and cypress mingle with the tears we shed.

▲ ① The Vacant Chair was written in 1861 for the American Civil War, but was adopted in Britain for the First World War. It was also set to music. At the same time, soldiers at the Front sang sentimental songs such as "It's a Long Way to Tipperary" (written in 1912), "Keep the Home Fires Burning" and "Bless 'em all". They all concentrated on the longing for home.

The Somme

All battles are awful, but some are more awful than others. One of these was called the Battle of the Somme.

The Somme is the name of a river in northern France. The first day of the Somme offensive was the bloodiest in the history of the British Army (picture ①). More than 20,000 were killed and 60,000 injured. Sixty per cent of all the officers were also killed on the first day.

The reason for the battle was that the British and French were trying (yet again) to break through the German lines. It was intended to be the winning battle. It was not – and two more wearying years of war followed.

The idea

In the northeast of France is a region called Flanders (picture ③, page 29). The battle line ran north to south through Flanders, British and French to the west, Germans to the east.

The countryside of Flanders is very flat and the ground is soft and often waterlogged. It is good trench-digging country, but there is no other shelter from attack.

The French plan was to attack from the south, but to confuse the Germans there would be a British attack from farther north to act as a diversion. However, there was a problem. In an earlier battle for the city of Verdun the French had suffered so many casualties that, when the attack was launched it was the British who ended up being the main attacking force.

Bombardment

The Battle of the Somme shows you how most battles of the First World War were fought.

It began on the 1st of July 1916, with an eight day **BOMBARDMENT**, known as 'softening up', which meant that the British heavy guns fired almost without pause, day and night, for eight days (picture ④).

They fired nearly 1.7 million shells. The idea was that they would 'lay a carpet of shells', as it was called, and completely smash the German trenches. However, it was not easy to fire shells accurately and so they did not succeed in doing this. Of course, the Germans knew what was going to happen and they shelled back.

Over the top

After the softening up, the infantry (foot soldiers) was commanded to go over the top. It was almost suicide. For ten weeks they tried to push forwards, but could make no advance.

Stalemate again

So next they tried using tanks (picture ②). This was the first time tanks had been used in battle. But of course, this was the early days of motor transport and half the tanks would not work. Nevertheless, they did help a little and showed that here was a weapon that could make a difference. But all the same, the stalemate continued.

At the end of the battle, on the 18th of November, just 10km of land had been won at the cost of one million casualties.

▼ ② **A First World War tank.**

► ③ Flanders was the scene of many battles, and in the end it was simply a sea of craters and stinking ponds. Here you see British reinforcements heading for the Front over a makeshift bridge.

▼ ④ A British heavy gun in action.

Poison gas

When you are desperate and indescribably tired, you are tempted to do some unspeakable things. The use of poison gas was one of these.

You may think of war as a battle with bullets, shells and bombs. But there is another kind of war using chemicals. It was first used by all sides in the First World War. It was the use of poison gas (picture ②).

What is poison gas?

We breathe in gases to live. Gases mix easily in the air, so if a poison gas is added to the air it is easy for it to affect large numbers

◀ ① Wearing gas masks.

▼ ② Going into battle amidst a cloud of poison gas.

▲ ③ If poison gas didn't kill, it often blinded and also brought the skin out in huge blisters.

of people. You may have heard of tear gas which is sometimes used in crowd control. This is a mild gas. The gases used in the First World War were far more deadly, although they blinded far more people than they killed (picture ③). The gases used included mustard gas (whose name comes from the yellow colour of sulphur) and the deadly, but easily-made green-coloured gas, chlorine.

Use of chlorine and mustard gas

The Germans were the first to use chlorine gas. In April 1915 they set off chlorine flares, creating a grey-green cloud that drifted over the French trenches. The French were forced to run away from it.

The French then used phosgene. This gas is invisible.

The most widely used gas was mustard gas, which caused horrible suffering and slow death.

Countermeasures

The most effective countermeasure was to wear a gas mask (picture ①). The mask had to cover eyes as well as nose and mouth because the gas could dissolve in tears in the eyes.

31

The first war in the skies

Aircraft were just a few years old when they were called into battle.

The first aeroplane was flown by the Wright Brothers in 1903. It stayed up for 12 seconds and flew 40m. But, quite remarkably, aircraft design improved by leaps and bounds. By 1909 Bleriot had crossed the English Channel. In 1911 the Italians, who were fighting Turkey at the time, dropped hand grenades from planes, making this the first use of an aircraft in war.

Not surprisingly, when war broke out there were hardly any aircraft, but they were so vital that many thousands were built (picture ①). France, for example, had 140 aircraft at the start of the war, but during the war France built 68,000 aircraft, although three-quarters were lost in battle. Being a pilot above the battle proved to be even more dangerous than being on the Front in a trench.

Although planes were too light to carry anything but the tiniest bombs (picture ③), they did carry machine guns which could be used to fire at ground troops or attack other aircraft. Battles between planes were known as dog fights. Planes were also able to drop leaflets on the people below, suggesting they should surrender, and the like.

Aircraft were also used to spy out for the troops, who could not see over their trenches.

Airships

Airships – vast balloons filled with hydrogen gas and with a little basket underneath – had been invented earlier than aeroplanes and they were also used in the war. They were able to drop bigger bombs.

The most famous airships belonged to Germany and were called Zeppelins. They made a bombing raid on London during the night of the 31st of May, 1915 (picture ②) although these bombs did little damage.

▼ ① **An artist's drawing of the aircraft crews as heroes.**

▼ ② **A plaque commemorating a Zeppelin bombing raid in central London.**

THESE PREMISES WERE TOTALLY DESTROYED BY A ZEPPELIN RAID DURING THE WORLD WAR ON SEPTEMBER 8ᵗʰ 1915 REBUILT 1917

JOHN PHILLIPS GOVERNING DIRECTOR

▼ ③ Small bombs were dropped by pilots from their cockpits!

Britannia rules the waves

Even though most of the battles were fought on land, it was vital for both Britain and Germany to control the seas, because they each needed to get extra supplies by sea.

At the start of the war, people in Britain thought back to the great victories of admirals such as Nelson at the Battle of Trafalgar.

At the start of the war, Britain had the world's biggest battle fleet, and the British wanted to see it in action again. However, what the navy needed to do was very different to battles of the past. Their job was to stop supplies getting to Germany by sea. Germany had a much smaller navy and its job was, somehow, to destroy the British navy. As it happens, the navies fought very rarely. The reason for this is that the British navy was able to bottle up the German navy in its home ports. It was afraid to come out because the British ships were far more powerful.

For most sailors it was a war of boredom – until the 31st of May, 1916.

The Battle of Jutland

Jutland is part of Denmark, and the big battle of the war was fought just off Denmark's coast.

The German commanders needed extra supplies, so they ordered their fleet to go out and break the British **BLOCKADE** (picture ①).

Remember that this was the first war to use radio and telegraph signals. Military signals were, of course, sent in secret code,

but the British had broken the German code just before the battle started, so they knew what the Germans were about to do.

The British fleet steamed off to block the Germans, and the fleets met just off Jutland. Altogether some 250 ships prepared to do battle. The battle began in the afternoon and lasted into the night. At that point the Germans decided they could not break through and retreated to their ports. They never came out again.

The battle cost Britain 14 ships and 6,000 men, while the Germans lost 11 ships and 2,500 men. These were tiny numbers compared to the losses on land. But the result was a victory for Britain because Germany could not get its supplies.

▼ ① **Here you see the British Grand Fleet sailing in formation. At this time all battle fleets steamed in short parallel lines. It was a very impressive sight. They had to stay close because the only way of passing messages between most ships was by flags or light flashes. Radio had not yet come into use. When battle began they formed into a single line. Each force tried to sail across the path of its enemy. Whoever did this could fire broadsides at the enemy, while the enemy could only fire with their front guns. The British admiral succeeded in doing this twice during the battle of Jutland.**

The first submarines

Germany then tried another way of winning at sea – it was the first country to use submarines. This seemed a brilliant idea at first. The German submarines were able to sink many British cargo ships (picture ②) and Britain was also getting seriously short of food. But eventually it was to cost the Germans the war. How it did so you can read on page 40.

▲ ② **A German submarine sinking British cargo ships.**

The Home Front

The war affected people at home, just as much as on the front line. The effort people made at home was vital. This is why it became known as the Home Front.

As more and more men went off to the Front, so the number of men left to work at home dwindled. In some places there were only women, children and the elderly. The exceptions were skilled people, who were needed to help the war effort at home (picture 1).

Factories still had to produce guns, shells and all the other materials needed for war, and farms still had to produce the food that everyone needed (picture 2), and as there were few men to do these jobs, women had to take their places. Food had to be sent to the troops on the Front, as well, and this was almost more than the country could provide.

Food **RATIONING** was introduced, so that everyone got the same basic foods needed to keep them healthy. Many luxuries disappeared. But Britain had depended on getting much of its food from its colonies, for there was only so much people could grow at home. The threat of running out of food was very real. Of course the Germans knew this, and that is why they tried to use submarines to sink British ships.

Women and the war

Before the war most women worked only at home. They did not have jobs that brought in wages. Of those that were working, most

▲ ① **Skilled men making wings for the new fighter aeroplanes.**

▲ ② Scouts digging land for planting.

▶ ③ Women delivering milk.

▼ ④ Women serving in shops.

women were servants and lived in the houses where they worked.

The fact that women had to do jobs that men had done before changed Britain for ever (pictures ③ and ④). Women gave up being servants in houses and working only at home and took factory and farm jobs. They would never go back to being servants again. Many others took up clerical jobs working for the government.

However, you must understand that this was a world very different from that we are used to today. Women still did not have the right to vote (although the **SUFFRAGETTES** were trying to change this) and after the war married women were banned from many jobs so that men had jobs to come back to. It would only be common for women to work in the years after the Second World War, thirty years later.

War spreads around the world

The war started in Europe. But most European countries had colonies, so they quickly got dragged in, too.

▲ (1) **Russian soldiers on the Eastern Front.**

The major countries involved in the First World War all had allies, interests and colonies spread around the world. From these came men and material that they used to fight the war.

The Eastern Front

About 4 million men faced one another across the trenches in the Eastern Front. It was the coldest kind of war, but the Russians (picture (1)) were more used to it than the Germans. Yet other things were happening. The Russians were becoming fed up with their rulers and with war, and in 1917 the **RUSSIAN REVOLUTION** took place. In this year **COMMUNISM** began and, as a result, the Russian army stopped fighting and Germany

was able to force peace terms on them and take large areas of territory. Russians would remember this in the Second World War.

Turkey

Outside Europe, two of the major campaigns were the Gallipoli campaign in Turkey and the battle for Palestine in the Middle East.

The attack on Turkey began as the British forces tried to find a way around the German trenches in Europe. Could there be a backdoor way in through Turkey, Germany's ally?

Allied forces tried to take the area near to the port city of Constantinople

▼ ② **Turks at the Jaffa Gate of Jerusalem in Palestine. Events in the First World War would eventually lead to the collapse of the Turkish Empire and the founding of the state of Israel.**

(now called Istanbul). But the Turkish guns were too powerful and the British ships could not land their troops properly.

The battles that occurred made up the campaign known as Gallipoli and they were a disaster for the allies. It cost 600,000 casualties and at the end the allies had to withdraw. Nothing was achieved.

Middle East

The Middle East had two great treasures: oil and the Suez Canal. The Germans and Turkish forces tried to capture the Suez Canal, which was British territory. Thirty thousand Indian army troops were sent to the canal's defence. Indians, helped by Australians, fought the attack off.

Meanwhile the British and Indian troops were sent to Mesopotamia (now Iraq) but the allied forces soon suffered another defeat at the hands of the Turks. But they tried again, and this time they captured Iraq, which then became British territory along with Palestine (picture ②).

Lawrence of Arabia

The British did not fight in Arabia, which was under Turkish control, but they helped the Arabs by giving assistance and leaders. The most famous leader was Colonel T.E. Lawrence – soon to be the famous hero, Laurence of Arabia. For two years Lawrence and his band of Arab tribesmen successfully attacked Turkish positions.

Weblink: www.CurriculumVisions.com

America enters the war

The war in Europe was a stalemate – until the United States entered on the side of Britain.

To understand about the United States, you have to know that almost all Americans come from immigrant backgrounds. There are Russian Americans, German Americans, Irish Americans, British Americans, Italian Americans, and so on. Indeed, in the middle of the 19th century there had actually been a vote to decide whether English or German should be the official language of America.

So, for the Americans, entering the war and taking sides was not an easy decision. Far better, they thought, to stay out of it, to stay neutral.

On top of this, America had been through a civil war not so many years before and it had fought for independence from Britain only a little over a century earlier.

But there was more. The president, Woodrow Wilson, was a pacifist, which means he did not believe in war. So, for three years, America stayed on the sidelines. To make it enter the war, one side or another in Europe had to do something to anger the Americans.

The President of America tried to get the governments of Europe to stop the war without a victory. But some Americans were already fighting as volunteers in the British army and these people returned with tales of daring and heroism, and of British sacrifice and German atrocities.

Yet it was none of these things that changed America's mind. It was an unbelievably stupid German 'own-goal'.

Sinking of the Lusitania

Remember that the Germans had started using submarines. The Americans were not at war, so they believed their ships would be left alone – including ships of other nations carrying Americans.

▲ ① **Propaganda poster reminding the American Government (shown as Uncle Sam in the front) of the death of American children due to the monstrous Germans (shown as the Kaiser at the back)**

However, the German government gave the order to sink any ship that approached Britain.

In 1915 a German submarine attacked and sunk a passenger liner sailing from New York to Britain. It was called the Lusitania (pictures ① and ②). More than 1,000 people died, including 138 Americans.

Americans were shocked, and for a while Germans stopped attacking American ships. Then, in January 1917 they resumed attacks on civilian ships – including American merchant ships.

Worse was to follow. In February 1917, Britain gave the American government a telegram they had obtained in which the German government asked the German ambassador to suggest to the Mexicans that they join Germany in attacking America. In exchange, once Germany had won the war, they would give Mexico all of her former territory that was now part of America.

The telegram was made public and instantly the mood in America changed. People now demanded war. On the 6th of April, 1917 the United States finally declared war on Germany.

▼ ② A painting of the sinking of the Lusitania.

By now the American government had also decided that sending American soldiers could end the war quickly, so it did not oppose the demands of the people.

At the same time, Germany was on the brink of starvation. Germany's allies, such as Turkey, were also collapsing.

The Americans arrive

The Americans arrived in force (picture ③). The United States, like Britain, entered the war with a small army, but it **DRAFTED** four million men in a few months and was soon sending ten thousand fresh soldiers (nicknamed 'dough-boys') to France every day. This was important, because all of the European soldiers were war-weary.

▼ ③ Americans arrive with more supplies.

The Americans were eventually persuaded to be part of a joint force. It was after this that the allies made their first advances against Germany (picture ④).

The final push began on the 8th of August, 1918. They advanced 12 kilometres into German-held territory in just seven hours. Soon advances were being made everywhere simply because Germany was overwhelmed thanks to the help of the American troops. Advances were even made in Flanders for the first time.

In four weeks of fighting over 100,000 German prisoners were taken, 75,000 by the British. The Germans realised they could not hold out any longer. In September they began to look for a peace treaty. Turkey signed an armistice on the 30th of October, followed by Austria-Hungary on the 3rd of November. On the 11th of November, Germany signed an armistice and all fighting ceased at exactly 11am.

▼ ④ **American troops throw hand grenades at a German position.**

Armistice, the final moment

Finally, on the 11th hour of the 11th day of the 11th month in 1918, the guns fell silent and the agreement to stop fighting was signed. This was called the ARMISTICE.

After the First World War, memorials were set up all over the world to remember those who had died (pictures ① and ②). The most famous is the memorial in Whitehall, the street near Parliament in London. The plain marble memorial represents a tomb of an unknown soldier. The memorial is called the Cenotaph. Here, each year, on the 11th hour, of the 11th day, of the 11th month, or the Sunday nearest to it, just as the last of the autumn leaves flutter down from the trees that line the road, the Queen and leaders from all over the Commonwealth, lay wreaths to remember those who were killed in the First World War, and the wars that have taken place since.

One of the most famous sentences of the war was written by Laurence Binyon as part of his poem, or ode, called "For the Fallen", which was written in 1914. It is used by the Royal British Legion and others at every remembrance ceremony:

> "They shall grow not old, as we that are left grow old;
> Age shall not weary them, nor the years condemn
> At the going down of the sun and in the morning
> We will remember them."

Here is where the verse fits into the full poem:

They went with songs to the battle, they were young.
Straight of limb, true of eyes, steady and aglow.
They were staunch to the end against odds uncounted,
They fell with their faces to the foe.
They shall grow not old, as we that are left grow old:
Age shall not weary them, nor the years condemn.
At the going down of the sun and in the morning,
We will remember them.

We will remember them.

▼ ② A war cemetery on Flanders Field as
it looked just after it had been established.

After the war

The UK lost 885,000 soldiers, 109,000 civilians and 1,663,435 wounded. The British Raj lost 74,000. New Zealand, with a population of just 1,100,000 lost 18,000 men and 41,000 wounded. In Germany, almost one in ten people were killed or wounded.

The war ended officially with the signing of the Treaty of Versailles on the 28th of June, 1919, but millions were still hungry, land was devastated and people were exhausted. And soldiers returning from the rat and lice infested trenches also brought something else home that winter – the flu. The flu that swept through an exhausted world in the winter of 1918–1919 would kill another 20 to 40 million people. Half the American deaths in the war, for example, were due to the flu and not enemy fire.

The largest price was paid by Germany, which was forced to accept blame for the war. The Germans lost all of their overseas territories and their entire navy, and were made to pay compensation that would bankrupt the country. All of these things, inflicted by the allies, would eventually lead to the rise to power of a man who fought as a lowly lance corporal in the First World War – Adolf Hitler.

So was it the war to end all wars?

No it was not. But the events that led to the Second World War are another long story, which you can find out about in these books:

Glossary

ALLIES A group of countries who are on the same side and who work together in time of war.

ARMISTICE An agreement to stop fighting. It usually comes before a peace treaty is signed.

BLOCKADE An attempt by one side to stop supplies arriving or leaving the enemy territory.

BOMBARDMENT A fierce and prolonged attack on an opposing force using shells or bombs dropped from aircraft which is designed to break the will of the opposition, destroy their guns, roads and so on. A bombardment usually comes before an attack using troops.

BRITISH EMPIRE The territories ruled directly by the British king or queen.

BRITANNIA A name originally given to the part that is now Great Britain ruled by the Romans. In the days of Queen Elizabeth I it was used as a name for a strong, almost goddess-like figure. In the times of Queen Victoria, she had a helmet, white robes, a three-pronged spear and stood in the ocean. She also had a shield with the Union Flag on it and a lion at her feet.

CIVIL WAR A war between two groups of the same country. Between 1861 and 1865 the northern states of the United States had been in civil war with the southern states over the issue of slavery.

COMMUNISM A way of living in which all property, factories and so on are owned by the people and where everyone is equal. A communist state is usually run by a group of unelected politicians.

CONVOY A group of ships or trucks that travel together for protection. They usually consist of cargo carriers and armed escorts.

DOMINION A dominion is a self-governing country that was once part of the British Empire, and which still has the British Queen as head of state.

DRAFT The word used in the United States for compulsory military service. In Britain the same thing is usually termed 'calling up'.

GANGRENE A very nasty illness in which the cells of the body that have been infected with a disease begin to die due to lack of blood supply. Gangrene can often only be dealt with by amputation.

MINE An explosive buried in a shallow pit in the soil and covered over to make it invisible. A small detonator sticks up from the mine. When pressure (foot or car tyre, for example) presses on the detonator, the mine is triggered.

RATIONING A system to share out essential scarce items evenly among people. Rationing is often organised with ration cards.

ROYAL BRITISH LEGION The United Kingdom's leading charity providing money and help to millions who have served, or who are currently serving, in the British Armed Forces, and their dependents.

RUSSIAN REVOLUTION A series of events in 1917 which overthrew the Czar (king) of Russia and replaced his government with the Communist Party.

STALEMATE A situation in which both sides are evenly matched and no-one can win.

SUFFRAGETTES A name for the women protestors in the early 20th century who campaigned for the right that women should be allowed to vote.

Index